- Self Care -

This Week Moto ______________________________

____

Self-Care Practices	Mon	Tue	Wen	Thu	Fri	Sat	Sun

- Self Care -

This Week Moto ______________________________

____

Self-Care Practices	Mon	Tue	Wen	Thu	Fri	Sat	Sun

- Self Care -

This Week Moto

Self-Care Practices	Mon	Tue	Wen	Thu	Fri	Sat	Sun

- Self Care -

This Week Moto

Self-Care Practices	Mon	Tue	Wen	Thu	Fri	Sat	Sun

- Self Care -

This Week Moto

Self-Care Practices	Mon	Tue	Wen	Thu	Fri	Sat	Sun